Beginning

HOCKEY

Coach Mike Foley and the following
athletes were photographed for this
book:
  Mike Brown,
  Mark Foley,
  Michael Kozlowski,
  Tim McManus,
  Heather Murphy,
  Marisa Pettiford,
  Robb Pottle,
  Travis Prunty,
  Tony Rocha,
  Chad Taylor.

Beginning
HOCKEY

Julie Jensen

Adapted from Mike Foley's
Fundamental Hockey

Photographs by Andy King

Lerner Publications Company ● Minneapolis

JUL 1997

Copyright © 1996 by Lerner Publications Company

Library of Congress Cataloging-in-Publication Data

Jensen, Julie, 1957–
  Beginning hockey / Julie Jensen ; adapted from Mike
Foley's Fundamental hockey ; photographs by Andy King.
    p.   cm. — (Beginning sports)
  Includes index.
  Summary: An introduction to the sport of ice hockey,
including its history, equipment, techniques, and terminology.
  ISBN 0–8225–3506–8 (alk. paper)
  1. Hockey—Juvenile literature. [1. Hockey.] I. King, Andy,
ill. II. Foley, Mike. Fundamental hockey. III. Title.
IV. Series.
GV847.25.J45   1995
796.962—dc20
                                            95–9920
                                                CIP
                                                AC

Manufactured in the United States of America

1 2 3 4 5 6 – HP – 01 00 99 98 97 96

Photo Acknowledgments
Photographs reproduced with permission of: pp. 7, 8 National Archives of Canada (neg. # C1007, C81683); p. 9, ALLSPORT/Steve Powell; p. 11, Courtesy of the Los Angeles Kings; p. 42, Courtesy of the Las Vegas Thunder; pp. 70, 73 (left), ALLSPORT/Jed Jacobsohn; p. 71, Mick Fletten; p. 72, Ringette Canada; p. 73 (right), Sledge Hockey Canada. All diagrams by Laura Westlund.

Contents

Chapter 1

How This Sport Got Started

More than a million people all over the world play the fast and exciting game called ice hockey. We don't know where and how hockey began, but we do know that it was played in England as early as the 1820s. By the late 1800s, Canadians were playing hockey too. The Ontario Hockey Association was founded in 1890.

One of the first hockey games in the United States was played in 1893. A team from Yale University played a team from Johns Hopkins University. Teams from Canada and the United States began playing professional hockey in the International Hockey League in 1904. The league lasted only three years.

The First Stanley Cup

The Governor General of Canada in 1893 was a hockey fan. Lord Stanley of Preston gave a trophy to the champion of the Amateur Hockey Association of Canada. The Stanley Cup has been awarded every year since 1893. The Stanley Cup is now given to the champion of the National Hockey League.

Early hockey players played on frozen ponds and outdoor rinks. This photograph was taken in about 1880 at McGill University in Montreal, Quebec.

Other professional leagues soon started. In 1917 the National Hockey Association and the Pacific Coast League combined to form the National Hockey League (NHL). At first, only teams from Canada played in the NHL. The Boston Bruins joined the NHL in 1924 and other U.S. teams soon followed.

Some of the best hockey players in the world play in the National Hockey League. Every spring, the NHL teams compete for the Stanley Cup Championship. Millions of people watch the final play-off games to see which team will win.

Some fans like to play hockey as much as they like to watch others play. Boys and girls in the United States can play in community hockey programs. Your local recreation center director can tell you what's available in your community.

Youngsters who are 4 to 8 years old play in beginner programs that are called Initiation Programs. The older players are divided into age groups:

Termites . . ages 5 and 6
Mites. . . . ages 7 and 8
Squirts . . . ages 9 and 10
Peewees . . . ages 11 and 12
Bantams . . . ages 13 and 14
Midgets . . . . ages 15 and 16
Juniors . . . . ages 17 and 18

An Olympic Miracle!

Do you like to cheer for an underdog? Many Americans did during the hockey competition at the 1980 Winter Olympics at Lake Placid, New York.

The U.S. team was rated the seventh-best team going into the 1980 Olympics. No one thought the Americans would win a medal. No one, that is, except U.S. Coach Herb Brooks.

The other teams had many older, more experienced players. Coach Brooks had the youngest team in Olympic history. But his college kids surprised some of the other teams and defeated them. To everyone's amazement, the young Americans soon were facing off against the powerful Soviet Union team in the semifinal game. Excited fans jammed every corner and aisle in the Lake Placid arena.

The young U.S. team scrapped and struggled to keep up with the Soviet squad. Midway through the third period, the score was tied 3-3. Red, white, and blue flags waved in the arena. Chants of "U.S.A. . . . U.S.A. . . . " filled the air.

Then Mike Eruzione, a youngster from Winthrop, Massachusetts, fired a shot past Soviet goaltender Vladimir Myshkin. The Americans were ahead, 4-3! Led by goal-tender Jim Craig, Team USA held on for the stunning victory. As the final seconds of the game ticked away, the television announcer asked, "Do you believe in miracles?" Many fans answered, "Yes!"

After the thrilling semifinal victory, Team USA played Finland in the championship. The Americans won, 4-2, to win the 1980 gold medal.

Chapter 2

BASICS

Ice hockey is the fastest sport in the world. Teams of six players, all on skates, race up and down the ice. The players use long, slender sticks to hit a hard rubber **puck**. Sometimes, the puck goes faster than 100 miles an hour. Hockey players even go in and out of the game without waiting for the action to stop. That's fast!

The object of all this effort is to put the puck into the opponent's **goal**. When a team does this, it scores a point. That point is also called a goal. The team with the most points at the end wins the game. A game is divided into three periods, with short rests between periods.

The Great One's Goof-up

Wayne Gretzky is the NHL's leading scorer. His nickname is "The Great One." He led the Edmonton Oilers to several Stanley Cup Championships. Now he plays for the Los Angeles Kings.

When Wayne was 13 years old, he and his dad decided to build a pair of hockey nets. They worked on them for days in their basement. Finally, they lifted the goal frames and began to carry them outside. They had a problem, however. The nets were too large to fit through the basement door. Wayne and his dad had to cut them into three pieces!

11

The Rink

Hockey is often played indoors. Large cooling systems keep the indoor ice frozen. A typical **rink** is 200 feet long and 85 feet wide. **Boards** that are 42 inches high surround the rink. Strong plastic extends another 5 to 8 feet from the top of the boards. The boards and plastic protect spectators and keep the puck in the rink.

The **red line,** also called the center line, divides the rink in half. The center **face-off** circle is in the middle of the red line. Play begins at the center face-off circle at the start of each period and after a goal has been scored.

At each end of the rink is a red **goal line** that stretches across the rink. At the middle of the goal line is a goal. A hockey goal has a steel frame. Heavy nylon mesh netting stretches between the goal posts and crossbar. The goalmouth is 6 feet wide by 4 feet high. A 6-foot light blue semicircle in front of the goal is outlined in red. This area is the **goal crease**. Players aren't allowed in their opponent's goal crease unless

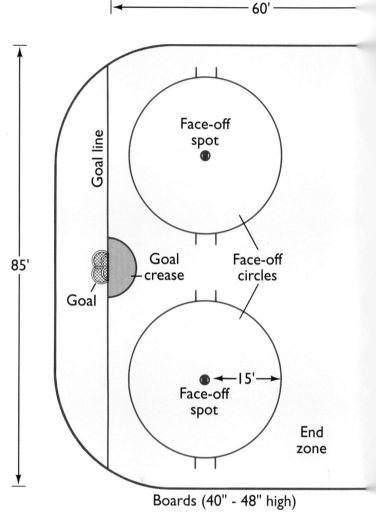

The Rink

the puck is already there.

Two **blue lines** divide the area between the goal lines into three zones. The **neutral zone** is the zone in the middle of the rink. A team's goal is in its **defending zone**. The other end zone is that team's **attacking zone**, or offensive zone.

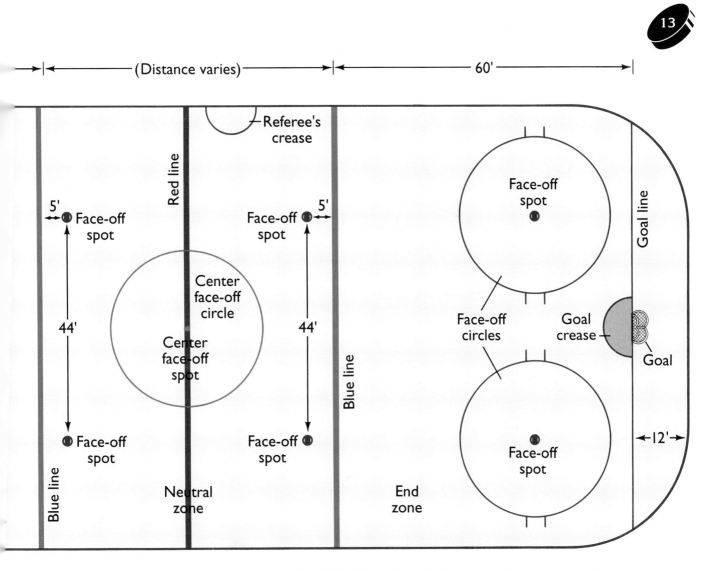

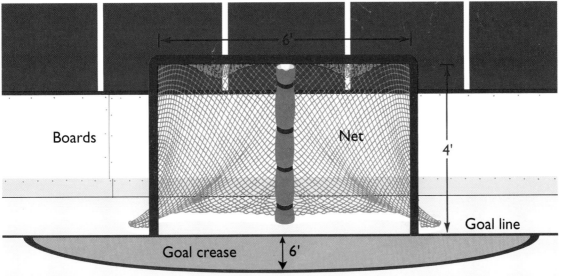

The Goal

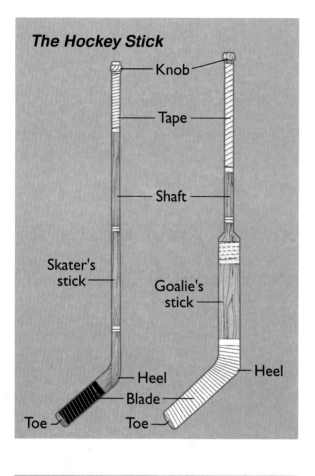

The Hockey Stick

Knob

Tape

Shaft

Skater's stick

Goalie's stick

Heel

Heel

Blade

Toe

Toe

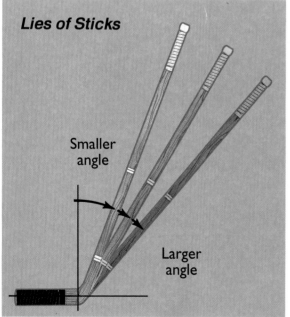

Lies of Sticks

Smaller angle

Larger angle

The Equipment

Most hockey equipment is designed to protect the players. Shin pads and padded pants called breezers protect a player's legs. Shoulder pads and elbow pads cover the arms and shoulders. Gloves protect the wrists and hands. Each player also wears a helmet with a face mask and a mouth guard.

One piece of equipment isn't for protection. That's the hockey stick. Most sticks are made entirely of wood, usually ash. Some sticks have an aluminum shaft with a wooden blade. A player holds the stick by its shaft and hits the puck with the blade.

If you are a right shooter, you place your right hand one-third of the way down the shaft and hold the end of the stick with your left hand. If you are a left shooter, you do the opposite. The angle at which the blade meets the shaft is called the **lie** of the stick. The smaller the angle, the easier it is to control the puck when it is close to you. But with a larger angle, you can control the puck over a bigger area.

One player needs different

equipment. The **goaltender,** or goalie, tries to keep the puck from entering his or her team's goal. A **save** is a shot that the goalie stops from going into the goal. Saves and goals are both called **shots on goal**.

A goaltender wears padded skates, large leather blocker pads, and breezers. A goalie also wears a chest protector, a blocking glove, a catching glove, and elbow, arm, and shoulder pads. A face mask and mouth guard complete the goalie's outfit. The shaft of a goaltender's stick is narrow at the top. The shaft widens into a paddle at the blade. Now that we know what hockey players wear, let's see what they do at a practice.

Stretching and Warm-up

First, the players stretch their muscles. Then they begin skating. The players skate slowly to warm up. Then they speed up. Finally, they skate at top speed.

Power Skating

The players then practice **power skating**. They keep their knees bent, hips low, chins up, and chests out for balance. Travis shows good power-skating form.

He turns his right skate out for the power thrust, or push. As he pushes off his right skate, Travis points his left skate straight ahead and glides on it. Then, he brings his right skate up to the heel of his left skate. He keeps his right skate low and close to the ice. Travis's right skate becomes the glide blade. Then his left skate is the thrust blade.

When the players practice backward skating, they stay in good power-skating form. They keep their knees bent, hips low, chins up, and chests out.

Mike is the best backward skater on his team. He begins with his feet about shoulder width apart. He pushes off the inside edge of his right skate and glides on his left skate. Mike alternates sides, pushing and gliding.

Crossovers

Players must be able to turn to their right and left sides while skating forward or backward. They use the **crossover** stride to turn. Mike is doing a backward crossover below.

To do a backward crossover, Mike keeps his knees bent, hips low, chest out, and chin up. He is turning to his left, so he rides the outside edge of his left skate. Mike picks up his right skate and crosses it over his left foot. He places his left skate back on his left side to complete one stride.

Travis is doing a forward crossover. To turn to his left, he rides the outside edge of his left skate. Travis pushes off the inside edge of his right skate. He brings his right skate over his left foot. To complete the stride, he places his left skate back on his left side.

Learn to do all the skills to both your right and left sides. One way will probably feel easier than the other. You may have to practice more on the tougher side.

Puck Carrying

Some players are right shooters and others are left shooters. Mark, the skater shown here, is a left shooter. When he shoots, he has his right hand at the top of his stick. His left hand is his power hand. He puts it lower on the stick's shaft. Mark's left side is his **forehand** side. His right side is his **backhand** side.

A right shooter holds the top, or knob, of the stick with his or her left hand. The shooter's right hand is his or her power hand. It is about one-third of the way down the shaft. A right shooter's forehand side is his or her right side. The left side is a right shooter's backhand side.

Puck carrying is moving the puck on the ice. To practice puck carrying, Mark holds the stick at the top. He releases his left hand. Keeping the puck on his forehand side, he pushes the puck up the ice.

After several trips up the ice, he turns his stick blade to his backhand side and practices his backhand carry. He keeps his head up so that he can see the other players.

Forehand carry

Backhand carry

Ready position

Stickhandling

Next, the players practice their **stickhandling** to control the puck. Chad, at left, is in the ready position for stickhandling. His skates point straight ahead. His knees are bent.

Travis, at right, is doing the side-to-side dribble. He taps the puck back and forth in front of his body.

Below, Travis uses the forward-and-back dribble. He puts his stick to the side of his body. He pushes the puck away from himself. Then he brings it back.

Forward-and-back dribble (photo above and bottom two photos on next page)

Side-to-side dribble: Travis brings the puck from his right side, across his body, to his left.

For the diagonal dribble, Travis moves the puck from his right to left. He moves it in a diagonal line, not straight across his body.

Good stickhandlers use all three of these patterns to move the puck quickly. By controlling the puck, good stickhandlers can confuse their defenders.

Goaltending

All goaltending moves start from the basic stance. Goalies try to quickly return to the basic stance after making a save.

Robb, at right, is in the basic stance. His feet are together. His knees and waist are bent, and his chin and shoulders are up. Robb has his catching glove open and out to his side. He holds his stick in his blocking glove. Robb's stick blade is flat on the ice.

From the basic stance, Robb can drop to the **V save** position, below. His knees are together and his skates are far apart. He forms an upside-down V with his legs.

Basic stance

● Skate Save

When Robb moves his skate blade in a semicircle to stop the puck, he is making a **skate save**. He uses this move to stop pucks that are on the ice.

● Stick Save

Robb can also stop low shots with his stick blade. This is a **stick save**. When Robb stops a shot with his blocker pads, he's made a **pad save**. When he catches the puck, it's a **glove save**.

● *Deck Save*

A **deck save,** or stacked pads slide save, is a tricky move. Robb does a deck save to his stick side by sliding on that side. He puts one leg on top of the other and puts his catching glove arm on top. He stretches out his arm and stick as far as possible. He can do this save on both sides.

Seeing through a Screen

A goaltender is "screened" if players are blocking the goalie's view. To see when you are screened, bend down near the ice. When you are low, you can see through the players' legs.

● *Rebounds*

Sometimes, after Robb has made a save, the puck bounces off his equipment. It lands on the ice in front of the net. A loose puck like this is a **rebound**. Rebounds are great scoring chances for shooters. Robb tries to prevent rebounds by directing the puck to the corners.

Robb can also catch the puck and hold it until the referee blows his or her whistle. He can also keep the puck under his body until play stops. Holding the puck this way is called freezing the puck.

Shooting

Every player wants to get a **hat trick,** which means to score three goals in a game. To do that, a player has to be a good shooter.

● *Wrist Shot*

First, the players work on the **wrist shot**. Mike skates directly toward the net. He shoots from his forehand side. His feet are square to the net. His weight is on the skate toward the puck. His stick blade doesn't leave the ice.

Mike snaps his wrists as he shoots to make the shot fast and hard. Wrist shots are quick and accurate.

● *Backhand Shot*

Next, Tony practices a back-hand shot. He comes toward the net from the side, rather than straight ahead. He drops the puck to his backhand side. Then Tony turns his hips, shoulders, and arms as he shoots.

● *Snap Shot*

For a **snap shot,** Chad's feet point toward the puck, not the goal. He pushes off his back skate and shifts his weight to his front foot.

At the same time, Chad pushes the puck ahead of himself about 6 to 10 inches. Chad snaps his wrists and whips the stick blade to the puck for the shot.

● *Slap Shot*

To hit a **slap shot**, Mark puts his weight on his back skate. He draws his stick blade back to shoulder height. His head is over the puck. As Mark draws the stick through, he shifts his weight to his front skate and slaps the puck toward the goal.

Passing

To practice forehand passing, the players pair off. Partners face each other, about 15 feet apart. They keep the puck on their forehand sides and use their wrists to sweep the puck to their partners.

Keep your stick blade on the ice when you are waiting for a pass. Your stick blade is the target for the passer. Let your stick give, or move back slightly, as the puck hits it. Hockey players refer to this as having "soft hands."

The players also practice backhand passing. With the puck on their backhand side, the players use just their arm muscles to move the stick and pass the puck. For the backhand shot, the players use their hips and shoulders too. But a pass doesn't need the speed of a shot.

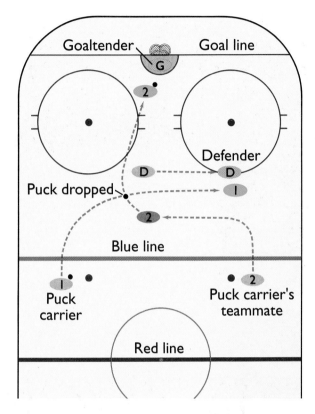

● Drop Pass

The diagram above shows how a **drop pass** is done. The puck carrier crosses the blue line. A partner also crosses the blue line, but stays behind the puck carrier. When the player with the puck is even with the defender, he or she stops the puck but continues skating. The defender continues to skate with the person who had the puck. The puck carrier's partner then picks up the puck and tries to score.

Checking

There are two kinds of checks. A **body check** means to use your body to bump the player who has the puck so that he or she loses control of it. A **stick check** means to use your stick to steal the puck from an opponent.

Some leagues don't allow body checking. Leagues that do are usually for players who are at least 13 years old.

● *Shoulder Check*

To practice a **shoulder check** Tony and Mark face each other. When the coach says "Now," Tony pushes off both skates. He drives his shoulder into Mark's chest area. Checkers keep their sticks on the ice, their feet wide apart, and their chins up for good balance.

A shoulder check can be used as a *takeout check*. A takeout check is any check that prevents a player from getting or keeping the puck. For example, when the puck is passed to Tony, Mark checks him against the boards. Mark's shoulder is in front of Tony and his leg is behind Tony. In this way, Mark takes Tony out of the play.

● Lift Check

A **lift check** is one kind of stick check. Marisa skates next to Heather, who has the puck. Marisa puts her stick shaft under Heather's stick. Marisa quickly lifts her stick and slaps the puck away from Heather. Marisa controls the puck and skates away!

● Poke Check

Another type of stick check is a **poke check**. Heather is the checker. She skates backward while facing the puck carrier, Marisa. Heather holds the stick with her top hand, and keeps it close to herself. This gives Marisa the idea that there is room to get the puck closer to Heather.

When Marisa gets close enough for Heather to reach the puck, Heather quickly thrusts her stick blade forward. She pokes away the puck and takes control of it.

Conditioning

Hockey players must be ready for bursts of intense activity in a game. They also must be able to play long, tiring games. Conditioning helps them prepare for these physical challenges.

At their coach's whistle, the players skate forward at full speed across the rink. Then they stop and sprint back to the starting point. They do this for two full minutes. After a minute of rest, they do three more two-minute bursts.

After the players have recovered, they skate forward around the rink to raise their heart and breathing rates. By doing this for 5 to 30 minutes, their heart and lungs become better at getting blood and oxygen to their bodies.

The Cooldown

Finally, the coach tells the players to slow down. They skate for three more minutes to cool down. Cooling down helps prevent muscles from cramping after all the hard work.

Chapter 3

GAME TIME

A hockey team has a **center,** a left **wing,** a right wing, a left **defenseman,** a right defense-man, and a goaltender. The center is the team's playmaker. The center usually leads the attack up the middle of the rink. Wings skate up and down the sides of the rink. They pass the puck to each other and to the center. Wings and centers are also called forwards.

Defensemen carry the puck out of their own end of the rink. They try to break up the plays of the opposing team. The goaltender's job is to keep the puck out of the goal. Goalies can skate anywhere on the rink, but most goaltenders stay in the goal crease or very close to it.

Ice Breaker!

Manon Rheaume (pronounced Ma-NOH Ray-OME) was the first woman to play professional hockey. She played goaltender for the Tampa Bay Lightning in a National Hockey League exhibition game in 1992.

Manon started skating when she was three years old. By the time she was five, she had already played in her first hockey game. Later, she played on the Canadian National Women's Hockey Team that won the 1992 World Championship.

Two wings and a center make up a **line**. Defensemen play in pairs. A team often has at least four lines, three defensive pairs, and two goaltenders. Players usually skate for only 60 to 90 seconds before being replaced by other players. A goaltender generally plays the entire game.

Face-offs and Penalties

Each period of a game begins with a face-off at the center face-off circle. Players line up on their team's side of the red line, on the short lines called **hash marks**. An official drops the puck between the two centers. The centers try to pass it to one of their teammates.

Face-offs are also used to restart play after a goal and after **offside** or **icing** violations. Offside is called when a player enters his or her team's attacking zone before the puck does. Icing is called when a player shoots the puck from his or her half of the rink so that it crosses the other team's goal line before another player can touch it. Where a face-off is held depends on where and why play was stopped.

For other violations, a player will be given a **penalty**. Players sit in the **penalty box** when they have broken a rule of the game.

When a player is in the penalty box, his or her team plays **short-handed,** or with fewer than six players on the ice. When a team is shorthanded, it is **killing a penalty**. Icing is legal for a team that is shorthanded. When one team is shorthanded, the other team is on the **power play**.

A **referee** is the chief official at a hockey game. The referee is in charge of the game and calls all the penalties. The other officials on the ice, called **lines-men,** watch for offside and icing. Off the ice, other officials record goals, watch the players in the penalty box, and run the game clock.

There are often just two on-ice officials for games at the beginning level. They serve as both referees and linesmen. As referees they call penalties, and as linesmen they watch for icing and offside. At high school and college games, there are often three on-ice officials.

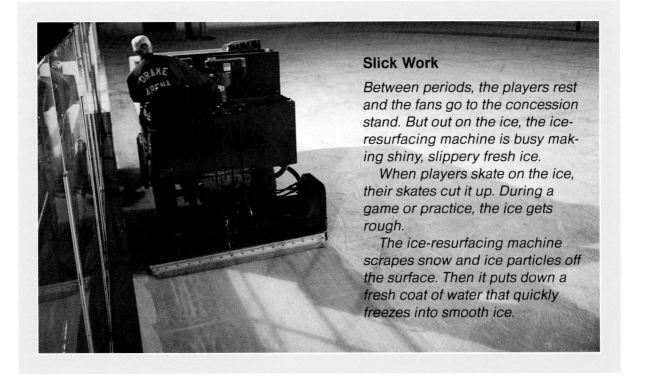

Slick Work

Between periods, the players rest and the fans go to the concession stand. But out on the ice, the ice-resurfacing machine is busy making shiny, slippery fresh ice.

When players skate on the ice, their skates cut it up. During a game or practice, the ice gets rough.

The ice-resurfacing machine scrapes snow and ice particles off the surface. Then it puts down a fresh coat of water that quickly freezes into smooth ice.

Playing the Game

Tony and Travis are teammates on their school team. During the summer, however, they play for different teams in a recreational hockey league. Tony is on the Rams. Travis plays for the Eagles. Let's see how they use their hockey skills in a summer league playoff game.

The Eagles win the opening face-off. Tom skates to the red line. He shoots the puck into the Rams' zone. Steve leads the **forecheck**. He goes to the opposing defenseman, who has the puck in the right corner. Tom skates to the boards on that side. Travis, his other linemate, is in front of the net. Both Eagle defensemen skate up and wait at the blue line.

The Rams are too quick, however. They complete a **breakout pass** and begin their attack up the ice. Three Rams are racing against two Eagle defenders. The Rams center cuts to the middle and leaves a drop pass for his linemate, Tony. Tony fires a quick, low wrist shot from the **slot**, and the Rams lead the Eagles 1-0!

The Rams skate for another 45 seconds. Then they go to the bench. The three players on the next line jump over the boards and go right into the play. This type of substitution is called changing **on the fly**.

When the first period ends, the Rams are still leading, 1-0. In the locker room, the Eagles coach tells them to start using their puck control system. The Eagles coach says, "Remember, we don't just throw the puck into their zone. If you come up the ice with the puck and there isn't an opening, turn and come back. Pass it back to our defensemen. We'll circle and regroup. Then we'll try again."

The Eagles coach also tells them to improve their **back-check**. The center and wings don't chase the puck carrier when they are backchecking. They follow the opposing center and wings. The defensemen cover the puck carrier.

Just 21 seconds into the second period, Travis shoots. The puck hits the goal post and caroms to the left corner of the rink. Travis wonders if maybe this just isn't the Eagles' day.

With six minutes left in the period, an Eagles defenseman gets a **breakaway**. As he skates in alone on the Rams goaltender, a Rams player trips him. The Rams player goes to the penalty box for a two-minute minor penalty. Now the Eagles are on the power play. They line up to the right of the Rams' net for the face-off. The Rams stand between their goal and the Eagles.

The Rams win the face-off. A Rams player shoots the puck the length of the ice. Icing isn't called because the Rams are killing a penalty. The Eagles hustle back to pick up the puck.

Darrin, an Eagles defenseman, starts the power play rush up the ice. At center ice, he passes to Travis. Travis carries the puck into the right corner of the Eagles' attacking zone. Steve is behind the net. Travis passes to him and then breaks for the goal crease. Travis calls for a return pass. A Rams defender follows Travis to the net. That leaves an open area on the right side. Darrin skates from the blue line into the open ice. Steve feeds him a near-perfect pass. Darrin's shot hits the upper right corner of the net. It's a tie game!

The Rams player leaves the penalty box, but soon the second period ends with the score, 1-1. In the locker room, the Eagles coach tells them to be patient and to stay with their game plan.

The Rams win the opening face-off of the third period. Tony shoots the puck deep into the Eagles' zone. The Rams have a new spark. They control the action but don't score.

Play is fast and exciting in the final four minutes of the game. Both teams get good scoring chances, but both goalies make key saves. At the end of the third period, the scoreboard still reads: Rams 1, Eagles 1.

A regular-season game can end in a tie, but a play-off game can't. The Rams and Eagles will play a five-minute overtime period. The game will be over as soon as one team scores a goal. That's pressure!

The players gather at their benches for a three-minute rest. The Eagles goaltender sits on the ice, leaning back on the boards. With his eyes closed, he concentrates on seeing himself moving in the goal crease and stopping the puck.

When the horn sounds to signal the end of the rest period, the players gather around their coach. He reminds them to take every shot on goal they possibly can.

Playing by the Rules

The rules of hockey are meant to keep the game safe and fair. Players are given a penalty and forced to sit in the penalty box when they have broken a rule. If a player is given a minor penalty, he or she must stay in the penalty box for two minutes or until the other team scores. For major penalties, the player must stay in the penalty box for a full five minutes, even if the other team scores.

A few coaches and players have given hockey a bad reputation by allowing rough play and fighting. Many of the best hockey players, however, including Wayne Gretzky and Mario Lemieux, have said over and over that fighting and hockey don't mix. It's that simple.

Here are some common violations:

- **Hooking:** *Using your stick to hold a player's arms, stick, or body.*
- **Slashing:** *Swinging your stick at an opponent.*
- **High-Sticking:** *Hitting someone above the waist with your stick, or touching the puck with your stick if the puck is more than 4 feet above the ice.*
- **Tripping:** *Using a stick, leg, or skate to cause another player to fall.*
- **Fighting:** *Punching or hitting an opponent. This results in the players having to leave the game.*
- **Unsportsmanlike Conduct:** *Swearing, gesturing, or doing anything inappropriate in athletic competition.*

Overtime Shooting

Most coaches tell their players to shoot often during overtime play. The coaches think that if their players keep the puck near the other team's goal, they will probably score. One successful coach had a simple rule for his players during overtime: Don't shoot unless you have the puck. Wayne Gretzky said it this way: "100 percent of the shots you don't take, don't go in."

After 55 seconds of the overtime period, the Rams and Eagles send fresh lines onto the ice. The Eagles control the face-off and take the puck into the Rams' zone. They get two shots and a rebound from close to the goal crease.

After the third save, the puck goes behind the Rams' net. Travis gains control of it. He fakes to his left. Then he uses a

wraparound shot to his right, sliding the puck between the goaltender's skate and the goal post. It's in the net! Travis's teammates pile on him in celebration. The Eagles win, 2-1! The Eagles and Rams shake hands at center ice.

Chapter 4

PRACTICE, PRACTICE

To play hockey well, you need to learn the basic skills. Once you learn those skills, the way to improve is by practicing. Just as you practice any other sport, or singing, dancing, or painting, if you practice your hockey skills you will improve.

Most coaches want their hockey players to practice all the skills, not just shooting. When you practice, be sure to work on skating, puck control and carrying, shooting, passing, and checking. And don't forget conditioning.

Scooter Drill

The scooter drill improves skating. Heather and Marisa point their left skates straight ahead. They push or "scoot" off their right skates again and again until they're at the other end of the rink. Then they go back, pushing off their left skates.

Agility Skating

Mark skates to the blue line and drops onto both knees. He glides on them and then gets up. Using his regular stride, he skates to the other blue line and drops to both knees again. Then he quickly gets back up.

Hockey Stops

To do a power stop on her front skate, Heather skates to the blue line. She shifts her weight to the inside edge of her front skate to stop. Then she pushes off that edge and returns to her starting place.

To change direction in a game, Chad uses the turning stop. He skates forward and stops on the outside edge of his back skate. His front skate is off the ice. He crosses his front leg over his back leg to complete the turn.

Targets in the Goal

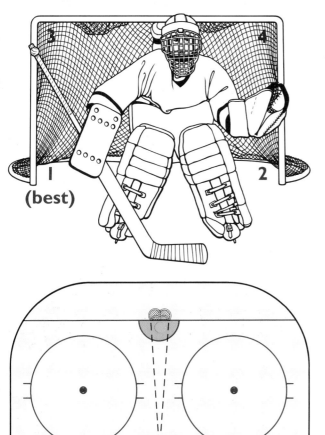

1 (best)   2

Percentage Shooting

When the players practice shooting, they shoot for the corners of the net. The corners are the easiest places to score.

They also remember the two things about shooting angles that are shown in the diagrams below.

Shooting Angles

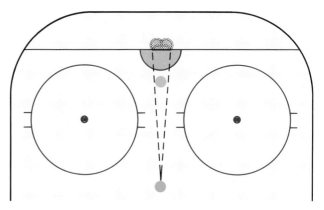

The closer the goaltender is to the goal, the bigger the target you have.

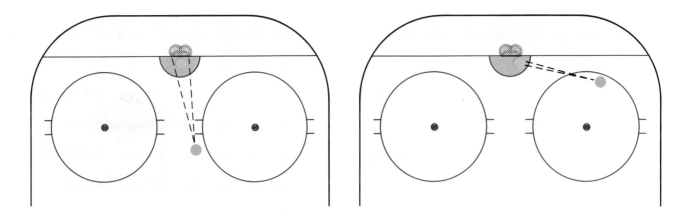

The closer you are to the center of the rink, the better your shooting angle.

Marisa is doing the "Easy drill." She starts at center ice and skates full speed to the blue line. Then she sets her skates at shoulder-width. She says aloud, "Easy Marisa . . . Easy Marisa . . . Easy Marisa . . . ," as she gets closer to the goal. Her arms are out, away from her body. The puck is at the tip of her stick blade. At about the hash mark, she snaps her wrists and flips the puck into the upper right corner of the net.

Checking It Out

To practice checking, the players pair off. One player is next to the boards. The other player is about two feet away. When the coach whistles, the players away from the boards check their partners. After several whistles, the players switch places. They try to always keep their heads up. That way, they won't be surprised by a check.

Practice is hard work, but it can also be fun. Coaches and players often don't have time on the ice to practice all the skills they would like to improve. But you can practice many hockey skills off the ice. This is called dryland training. You can practice alone or with your friends. You can wear gym shoes or in-line skates.

Practice your stickhandling and shooting on your driveway, garage, basement floor, or on any smooth, hard surface. Plastic pucks are useful for shooting practice. Tennis balls, golf balls, or roller pucks can be used for stickhandling practice.

Design a small obstacle course for yourself and your friends. Jumping, spinning, and moving quickly to your left and right sides will improve your speed, balance, and agility. Roller hockey, in-line skating, and rope jumping are also good dryland training methods.

Home Improvement

A dryland slideboard is a great way to improve your skating stride. You can build one with an adult's help.

First, get a piece of 1-inch thick plywood that is 2 feet wide by 8 feet long. Glue countertop material (such as Formica) to the board. Fasten two boards, 4 inches wide by 2 inches thick by 2 feet long, near each end of the first board.

Next, glue foam padding along the inside edges of the end boards. Spray the countertop material with silicone spray or baby oil. Put on clean athletic socks. Take your hockey stick, get on the board, and begin skating.

Chapter 5

RAZZLE DAZZLE

". . . He slides off the check. . . . He's in alone on goal. . . . He shoots. . . . He sco-o-o-o-ores! The Bruins take a two-goal lead with less than a minute to play."

Watching high school, college, Olympic, and professional hockey games can be fun. Just ask Travis, Heather, and the other players. You will see some of hockey's most advanced skills demonstrated by excellent players. Don't be discouraged if you can't master these flashy moves right away. Keep practicing. Someday, young hockey players will be watching you!

Hockey Camps

One way to improve your hockey skills is to attend a hockey camp. Before signing up for a hockey school or camp, ask some of these questions:

- *How many players are on the ice during instructional sessions? How many coaches are on the ice during instructional sessions? There should be at least one instructor for every 10 athletes.*

- *Who are the coaches? The coaches should be old enough to know how to help you improve. If some of the coaches are high school or college players, there should be an adult coach to supervise them.*

- *Is there a daily schedule? You should work on basic skills, conditioning, and skills special to your position.*

- *What is the total cost? Be sure to find out what isn't included in the cost, such as snacks, jerseys, or instructional materials.*

Slide-Through and Pickup

One move Tony has seen college players do is the slide-through and pickup. Tony is practicing a forehand slide-through with his coach. Tony skates forward with the puck on his forehand side. He dips his head to one side to make his

65

Passing Lanes

One lane for the slide-through and pickup is shown in the top photograph below. This lane is between the defender's legs. Another lane, shown in the bottom photograph, is under the defender's stick. This is the most effective lane.

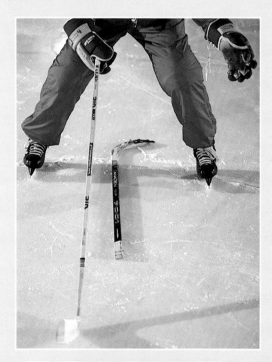

coach think he's going that way. Tony then slides the puck under the coach's stick and picks it up on his backhand side.

Trigger Shooting

Only a few of the best players can **one-time** a shot. One-timing, or trigger shooting, means to shoot directly off a pass without first stopping the puck. A shooter who can one-time a shot often catches the goaltender out of position.

As the puck comes toward Travis, his weight is on his back skate. His knees are bent. When the pass reaches Travis's stick, he pushes hard off his back skate. He shifts his weight to his front foot. Travis brings his stick blade through in a driving slap shot.

Board-Carom Passing

A **board-carom pass** can be to a teammate, as Mark and Chad demonstrate. Mark bounces the puck past a defender and off the boards to Chad. You can also pass to yourself when you're near the boards and an opponent is coming toward you.

Checking

Shoulder, poke, and lift checks are the basic checks. Here are some more advanced checks.

● *Sweep Check*

Mark is demonstrating a **sweep check**. As the puck carrier approaches, Mark drops to one knee. He holds his stick with just his top hand. Then Mark "sweeps" the stick in a half-circle, brushing away the puck. He quickly gets up and tries to control the puck.

● *Hip Check*

The **hip check** is the most difficult check in hockey. It requires excellent balance and timing. A hip check is used on open ice or along the boards.

Mark skates forward with the puck. As Mark moves around Tony, Tony bends at his waist and pushes off his back skate. Tony drives his hip into Mark.

MORE WAYS TO PLAY

Hockey is played in many ways. There are four-on-four games with four skaters and a goaltender on each team. There are even three-on-three games with three skaters and a goaltender on each side.

You can also play games like hockey without skating. For example, players wear rubber-soled boots instead of skates when playing boot hockey. Broomball players also wear boots. They use stiff-bristled brooms and a ball, rather than sticks and a puck.

Broomball is popular as an indoor and outdoor sport. Players wear boots and hit a ball with brooms.

71

Some girls choose to play ringette instead of hockey. The games are similar except for some of the equipment. Ringette players use long, straight sticks to control a doughnut-like puck.

Ringette is another game very much like hockey. Ringette players skate on a regular hockey rink. They use a stick without a blade to dribble, pass, and shoot a rubber ring at a goal.

Some games like hockey are played on surfaces other than ice. Field hockey is played on grass. Players wear gym shoes. They use short, curved sticks to hit a small, hard rubber ball. Floor hockey can be played in a gym or on blacktop or concrete. Players wear gym shoes and shoot a plastic puck with plastic or regular hockey sticks.

Roller hockey is an exciting new game off the ice. Roller hockey is most often played in a rink with boards. It can also be enjoyed on any large blacktop or concrete surface. Players wear in-line skates. They use regular hockey sticks and a special puck.

You can play ice hockey and its variations in many places. Your neighborhood recreation center or school physical education teacher should be able to help you find a place to play. If you want to learn how to play hockey, or if you already play and want to improve your skills, there are many hockey schools and camps you can attend. Choose the level that's right for you and get started!

Sledge hockey players use sleds instead of skates.

Sledge Hockey

"Sledge" is another word for sled. Players with lower-body disabilities use sleds to play sledge hockey.

Sledge hockey teams use six players at a time. Sledge hockey is played on a standard rink with a regulation puck, standard goals, and regular hockey rules. Players sit on sleds about three inches off the ice. The sleds have skate blades. The athletes push themselves around the rink and handle the puck using two sticks with ice picks on the bottom.

Sledge hockey began in Norway in 1967. More teams play sledge hockey every year.

HOCKEY TALK

attacking zone: The area of the rink surrounding the opponent's goal, bounded by a blue line and an end of the rink. Also called a team's offensive zone.

backcheck: A system for covering and checking opponents while they are bringing the puck up the ice.

backhand: A shot or pass in which the *back* of the puck carrier's bottom hand (power hand) is toward the target.

blue line: One of two 1-foot-wide blue lines that indicate where an offensive zone begins. A blue line is 60 feet from a goal line.

board-carom pass: A pass that is bounced off the boards to a teammate or to oneself.

boards: Sheets of lumber or hard plastic 3½ to 4 feet high that surround the rink.

body check: The act of using one's body to block or hit another player so that the other player loses control of the puck.

breakaway: A play in which the puck carrier faces only the goaltender.

breakout pass: A pass used by a team to move the puck out of its defensive zone.

center: The forward who plays between the two wings. Centers usually take face-offs.

crossover: A method of skating in which the skater alternates putting one foot across and in front of the other.

deck save: A save by the goaltender in which he or she stretches out flat on the ice on his or her side. Also called a stacked pads slide save.

defending zone: The area of the rink surrounding a team's goal, bounded by a blue line and an end of the rink. A team's defending zone is its opponent's attacking or offensive zone.

defenseman: One of two players on the ice whose primary responsibility is to help the goaltender protect their team's goal.

drop pass: A pass in which the puck carrier leaves the puck for a teammate trailing behind.

face-off: The act of dropping the puck between two opposing players to start or resume play. A face-off is held to start each period, after every goal, and after every stoppage of play.

forecheck: Pressure applied to the defensive team to prevent it from taking the puck out of its zone.

forehand: A shot or pass in which the *palm* of the puck carrier's bottom hand (power hand) is toward the target.

glove save: A save in which the goaltender catches the puck with his or her glove hand.

goal: An area 6 feet wide, 4 feet high, and 10 feet from the end of the rink that is defined by the crossbar and goal posts and the mesh netting stretched between

them. Also, the shooting of a puck over the goal line, between the goal posts and underneath the crossbar. Each goal is worth one point.

goal crease: The semicircle in front of the goal. Members of the attacking team aren't allowed in the goal crease unless the puck is in the crease.

goal line: A 2-inch-wide red line extending across the rink 10 feet from the end of the rink. The goal is placed in the middle of the goal line with the line at the front of the goalmouth.

goaltender (goalie): The player who stays near his or her team's goal and tries to keep the puck from entering it.

hash mark: One of several short lines around the face-off circles that designate where players should stand before the puck is dropped for a face-off.

hat trick: The scoring of three goals by one person in one game.

hip check: A body check in which the checker uses his or her hip to check the puck carrier.

icing: The act of shooting the puck from one's defensive side of the red line so that it crosses the goal line before a player other than the goaltender touches it. A team can legally ice the puck when it is shorthanded. In all other cases, icing results in a face-off in the icing team's defending zone.

killing a penalty: The defense used when a team is shorthanded because a player or players are in the penalty box and the opposing team is on a power play.

lie: The angle between the hockey stick's shaft and blade. The higher the number, the smaller the angle and the easier it is to control the puck close to one's body. The bigger the angle, the easier it is to control the puck farther from one's body.

lift check: A check done by using one's stick to lift an opponent's stick off the ice.

line: An offensive unit of two wings and a center who skate together.

linesman: An official responsible for calling offside and icing.

neutral zone: The area of ice between the blue lines.

offside: A violation of the rules that occurs when an offensive player enters his or her attacking zone before the puck or when a pass crosses a blue line and the red line before being touched by another player.

one-time: A method of shooting the puck after receiving a pass without stopping the puck first. Also called trigger shooting.

on the fly: A way of substituting players without stopping the game.

pad save: A save in which the goaltender uses his or her pads to stop the puck.

penalty: A punishment for breaking a rule. A minor penalty results in a player being in the penalty box for two minutes or until the other team scores. A major penalty results in a player being in the penalty box for five minutes even if the other team scores. A misconduct penalty results in a

player being in the penalty box for 10 minutes but his or her team doesn't have to play shorthanded.

penalty box: A small cubicle where players sit while serving a penalty.

poke check: A check that involves poking the puck away from the puck carrier with one's stick.

power play: The offense used when one's team has more players on the ice because the other team has a player or players in the penalty box.

power skating: A method of skating that involves powerfully pushing off one skate while gliding on the other. Power skating is the preferred method of skating for hockey players.

puck: A 3-inch-across, 1-inch-thick rubber disk.

puck carrying: Controlling the puck with one's stick.

rebound: A bouncing of the puck back into play after the goaltender makes a save and doesn't retain control of the puck.

red line: The 1-foot-wide red line that divides the rink in half.

referee: An official responsible for calling penalties and for the overall control of a game.

rink: A smooth area of ice. A rink can be inside a building or outside. A typical rink is 200 feet by 85 feet.

save: The prevention of a goal, usually by a goaltender using his or her glove, stick, pad, or skate.

shorthanded: A team with fewer players on the ice than its opponent is said to be playing shorthanded.

shot on goal: A shot that scores a goal or would have scored a goal if another player had not touched it.

shoulder check: A check in which the checking player uses his or her shoulder to bump the puck carrier.

skate save: A save in which the goaltender uses his or her skate to stop the puck.

slap shot: A shot in which the shooter draws back his or her stick to shoulder height before swinging and hitting the puck.

slot: An imaginary triangle defined by the goal and the inside edges of the face-off circles. The slot is considered the best place from which to shoot.

snap shot: A forehand shot in which the shooter hits the puck without first winding up. The shooter snaps his or her wrists to generate the power for the shot.

stick check: The act of using one's stick to take the puck away from an opponent.

stickhandling: Using one's stick to control the puck or steal the puck from an opponent.

stick save: A save in which the goaltender uses his or her stick to stop the puck.

sweep check: Taking the puck away from an opponent by dropping to one knee and sweeping one's stick flat on the ice.

V save: A save in which the goaltender drops to the ice on his or her knees with the knees together and the feet apart. Also called a butterfly save.

wing: A forward who plays on the left or right side.

wraparound shot: A shot in which the shooter starts from behind the goal and pushes the puck around one goal post.

wrist shot: A shot in which the shooter keeps his or her stick on the ice and generates the power for the shot by snapping his or her wrists.

FURTHER READING

Bertagna, Joseph. *Goaltending, A Complete Handbook for Goalies and Coaches.* Cambridge, Mass.: Cosmos Press, Inc., 1976.

Blase, Keith. *The AHAUS Coaches Checking Handbook.* Colorado Springs, Colo.: USA Hockey, Inc., 1986.

Blase, Keith. *The AHAUS Coaches Powerskating Handbook.* Colorado Springs, Colo.: USA Hockey, Inc., 1985.

Blase, Keith. *The AHAUS Coaches Puck Control Handbook.* Colorado Springs, Colo.: USA Hockey, Inc., 1986.

Burggraf, Nancy. *Stick Down Head Up!* Fargo, N.D.: Burggraf Skating Skills, Inc., 3129 9½ Street North, 1992. Training video and manual.

Falla, Jack. *Sports Illustrated Hockey: Learn to Play the Modern Way.* New York: Sports Illustrated Winner's Circle Books (Time, Inc.), 1987.

Foley, Mike. *Hockey, Play by Play.* Wayzata, Minn.: Turtinen Publishing, Inc., 1973.

FOR MORE INFORMATION

Canadian Amateur Hockey Association (CAHA)
16000 James Naismith Drive
Gloucester, Ontario, K1B 5N4
Canada

USA Hockey, Inc.
4965 North 30th Street
Colorado Springs, CO 80911

INDEX